VOCAL SELECTIONS

Junkyard Dog Productions

Stem Productions   Altar Identity Studios   Alex and Katya Lukianov

Susan and Jim Blair   Linda and Bill Potter

in association with

Yasuhiro Kawana   Vijay and Sita Vashee   Kevin and Lynn Foley   Jeff and Julie Goldstein

Edward and Mimi Kirsh   Frank and Denise Phillips   Steve Reynolds and Paula Rosput Reynolds   Land Line Productions

Alhadeff Family Productions/Sheri and Les Biller   Pat Halloran/Laura Little Theatrical Productions

Tony Meola/Remmel T. Dickinson and John Yonover   ShadowCatcher Entertainment/Tom and Connie Walsh

present

ZACHARY LEVI   KRYSTA RODRIGUEZ

FIRST DATE

Book by	Music and Lyrics by
AUSTIN WINSBERG	**ALAN ZACHARY & MICHAEL WEINER**

featuring

SARA CHASE   KRISTOFFER CUSICK   BLAKE HAMMOND   KATE LOPREST   BRYCE RYNESS

with

ERIC ANKRIM   KEVIN KERN   VICKI NOON   SYDNEY SHEPHERD

Scenic and Media Design	Costume Design	Lighting Design	Sound Design
DAVID GALLO	**DAVID C. WOOLARD**	**MIKE BALDASSARI**	**KAI HARADA**

Hair Design	Casting by	Assistant Director	Associate Choreographer
JOSH MARQUETTE	**TELSEY + COMPANY**	**BRANDON IVIE**	**LEE WILKINS**
	RACHEL HOFFMAN CSA		

Orchestrations	Conductor	Music Coordinator
AUGUST ERIKSMOEN	**DOMINICK AMENDUM**	**MICHAEL KELLER**

General Manager	Production Stage Manager	Production Management	Press Agent	Advertising and Marketing
ALCHEMY PRODUCTION GROUP	**ARTURO E. PORAZZI**	**JUNIPER STREET**	**THE HARTMAN GROUP**	**AKA**
CARL PASBJERG & FRANK SCARDINO		**PRODUCTIONS, INC.**		

Music Supervision, Vocal and Incidental Music Arrangements by

DOMINICK AMENDUM

Musical Staging by

JOSH RHODES

Directed by

BILL BERRY

Originally co-produced by The 5th Avenue Theatre

David Armstrong, Executive Producer and Artistic Director; Bernadine Griffin, Managing Director; Bill Berry, Producing Director and

A Contemporary Theatre, Seattle, WA

Kurt Beattie, Artistic Director and Carlo Scandiuzzi, Executive Director

ISBN 978-1-4803-6452-3

R & H THEATRICALS
229 West 28th Street, 11th Floor
New York, New York 10001
Tel 800/400.8160 or 212/564.4000 * Fax 212/268.1245 * E-mail theatre@rnh.com
Website www.rnh.com

IMAGEM MUSIC

EXCLUSIVELY DISTRIBUTED BY

HAL•LEONARD
CORPORATION

7777 W. BLUEMOUND RD. P.O. BOX 13819 MILWAUKEE, WI 53213

ALAN ZACHARY & MICHAEL WEINER met in high school where they first began to collaborate on musical and non-musical film, theatre, television and animated projects. Since then, their songs have been translated into over 25 languages, and they've developed properties for Warner Bros., 20th Century Fox, Universal, Hanna-Barbera, and numerous divisions of the Walt Disney Company, including: Disney Animation, Disney Channel, Disney Creative Entertainment, Disney Cruise Line, and Disney Parks & Resorts around the globe. Additionally, the duo has performed together at classic venues like the Duplex and 54 Below in New York, the Gardenia Club in Hollywood, and at the world-renowned Kennedy Center in Washington, D.C. as part of the "Broadway Today & Tomorrow" series, celebrating the present and next generation of Broadway songwriters. In 2012, they were presented with the ASCAP Foundation Richard Rodgers New Horizons Award by Broadway legend Stephen Schwartz.

In July 2013, after a sold-out run in Seattle, Zachary & Weiner's original romantic comedy musical *First Date* – with book by Austin Winsberg – began performances on Broadway at the Longacre Theatre, starring Zachary Levi and Krysta Rodriguez. And starting in 2014, *First Date* will have productions in countries spanning the globe. 2013 also saw the world premiere of *Secondhand Lions*, a Broadway-bound musical adaptation of the New Line Cinema film, with music and lyrics by Zachary & Weiner and book by Tony Award-winning Rupert Holmes, produced with Warner Bros. Theatre Ventures at Seattle's 5th Avenue Theatre. And the writing team's original stage musical *Twice Charmed* – which premiered on the Disney Cruise Line in May 2005 (cast recording on Walt Disney Records) – continues to be an audience favorite.

In the worlds of film, TV and online media, Zachary & Weiner have written songs for an animated musical feature at Amazon Studios, the script for an animated TV series for FOX, and developed a sitcom pilot at Disney Channel. They are also creators of *The Misadventures of Bob Paparazzo*, a comedy animated series for VH1 Online & Mobile. And you may have heard their irreverent theme song for Folgers coffee entitled "Happy Morning" which was featured in a popular viral marketing campaign that swept the Internet.

Separately, Alan Zachary contributed music and lyrics to DreamWorks Pictures' *The Time Machine*, and Michael Weiner composed the score for Fine Line Features' *Man of The Century* as well as the original stage musical, *Liberty Smith* (**www.libertysmith.com**), which has been seen at NAMT, NYMF and enjoyed a successful world premiere run in 2011 at Ford's Theatre in Washington, D.C.

For more info, please visit:
www.zacharyandweiner.com

Cast Shot - Sara Chase, Bryce Ryness, Zachary Levi, Kristoffer Cusick, Krysta Rodriguez, Blake Hammond, Kate Loprest © Chris Owyoung

That's Why You Love Me - Bryce Ryness, Krysta Rodriguez, Kristoffer Cusick © Chris Owyoung

Safer - Krysta Rodriguez © Joan Marcus

The Check - Kristoffer Cusick, Krysta Rodriguez, Sara Chase, Bryce Ryness, Zachary Levi, Kate Loprest, Blake Hammond © Chris Owyoung

The Girl For You - Bryce Ryness, Kate Loprest, Krysta Rodriguez, Sara Chase, Zachary Levi, Blake Hammond, Kristoffer Cusick © Chris Owyoung

Subway Shot - Krysta Rodriguez, Zachary Levi © Joan Marcus

The One - Bryce Ryness, Kristoffer Cusick, Zachary Levi, Krysta Rodriguez, Kate Loprest, Sara Chase © Chris Owyoung

First Impressions - Zachary Levi, Krysta Rodriguez © Joan Marcus

THE ONE

Music and Lyrics by
ALAN ZACHARY and MICHAEL WEINER

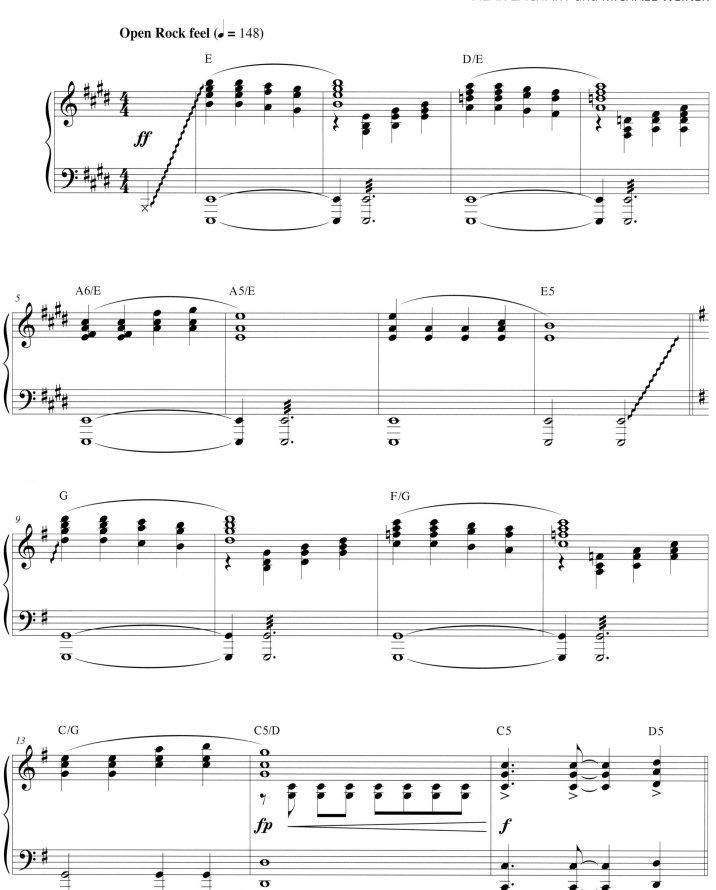

12

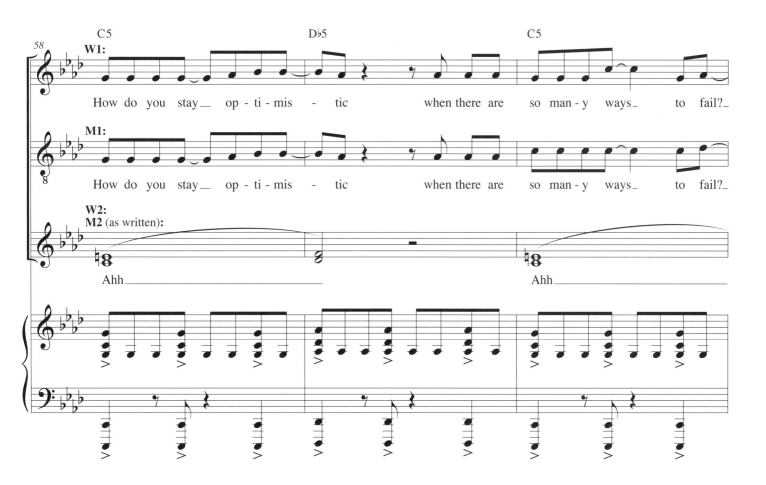

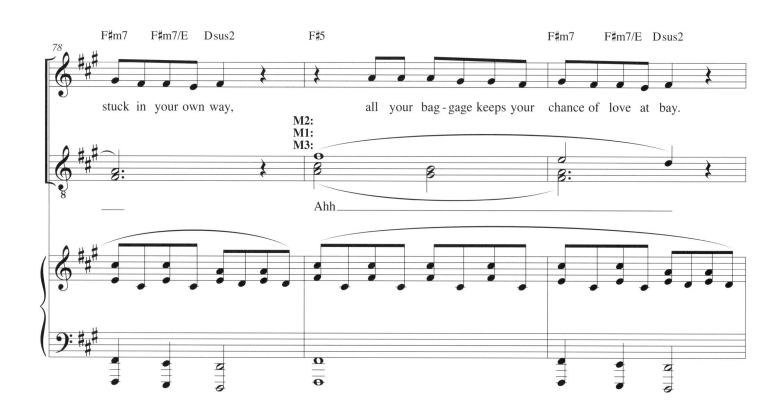

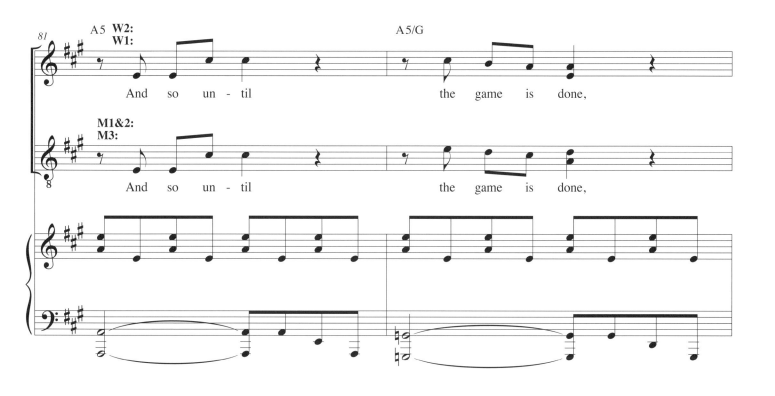

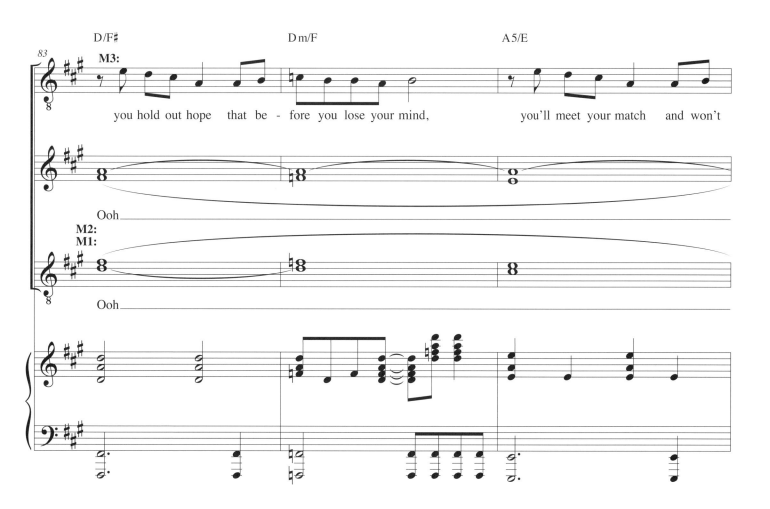

FIRST IMPRESSIONS

Music and Lyrics by
ALAN ZACHARY and MICHAEL WEINER

Funky, with motion (♩ = 150)

CASEY: *So, do you agree with Kevin?*
AARON: *About what?*

CASEY: *Am I "really cute"?*

AARON: *What? You can't just ask me that!*

CASEY: *Why not? You said you were an "open book." So... am I?*

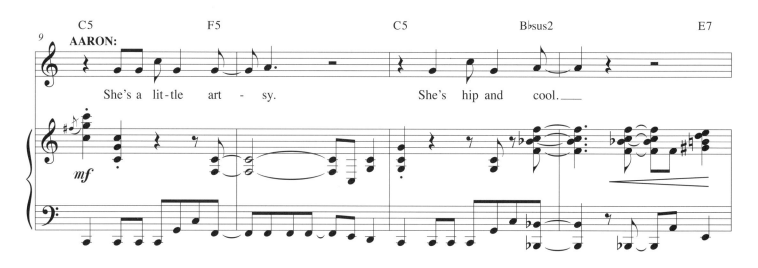

AARON:
She's a lit-tle art-sy. She's hip and cool.___

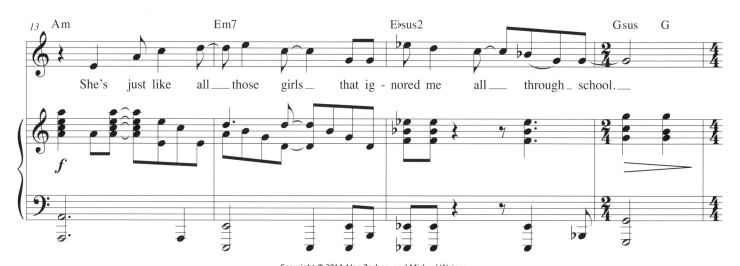

She's just like all___ those girls___ that ig-nored me all___ through___ school.___

CASEY: *I'm waiting?* **AARON:** *Uhm, yes. You're very... pleasant looking.*

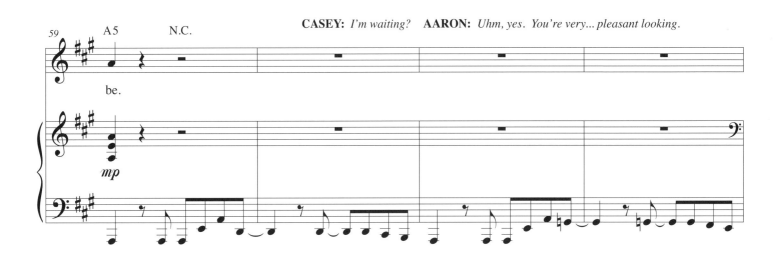

CASEY: *Pleasant looking?* **AARON:** *No, I mean—attractive? Desirable? Stunningly beautiful? How about "D,"*

(cont'd) **AARON:** *all of the above? And what adjectives would you use to describe me?*

CASEY: *Really—there's just so many adjectives to choose from. I wouldn't even know where to start.*

BAILOUT SONG #1

CASEY'S VOICE: *Hey, it's Casey. Blah blah blah blah blah…*

Music and Lyrics by
ALAN ZACHARY and MICHAEL WEINER

Lady Gagalicious (♩ = 175)

N.C.   Cm   A♭maj7

REGGIE:

This is your bail - out, sweet-ie, your bail - out, hon-ey, I'm

BACKUPS:

Bail - out!   Bail - out!

(Beep!)   *f*

G   Cm

call - in' to bail you out. You could tell him your dad's in the hos - pi - tal, your

Call - in' to bail you out!   Dad's in the hos - pi - tal, your

A♭maj7   Fm   E♭

build-ing's on fi - re. That's all you need to say, and you're

build-ing's on fi - re!

THE GIRL FOR YOU

Music and Lyrics by
ALAN ZACHARY and MICHAEL WEINER

AARON: *Should we continue playing Jewish Geography?*
'Cause I can give you like ten more names...

CASEY: *We can. I am good at this game. Even if I'm not a Jew.* [music]

AARON: *I'm sorry, what did you just say?*
CASEY: *I said, I'm not a Jew...*

38

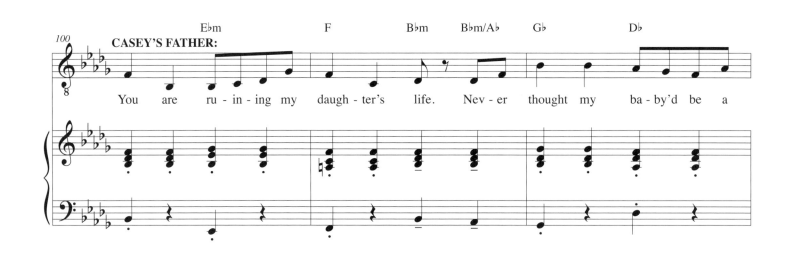

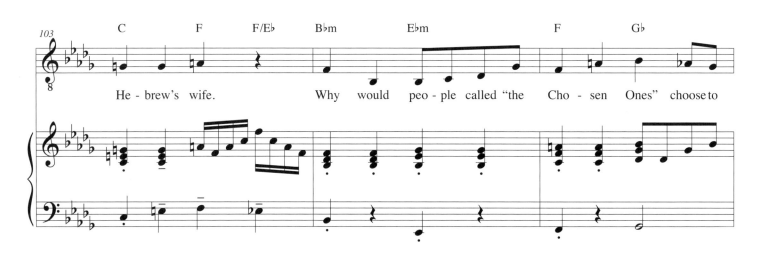

AARON'S FUTURE SON: *Yo, Dad. 'Sup?*
AARON: *Uhh, I'm sorry... "Dad"?*

AARON'S FUTURE SON: *What, you don't recognize me? I'm yours and Casey's future son. And I'm, like,* beyond *messed up. So—thanks for that...*

48

THE AWKWARD PAUSE

Music and Lyrics by
ALAN ZACHARY and MICHAEL WEINER

À la Simon and Garfunkel (♩ = 114)

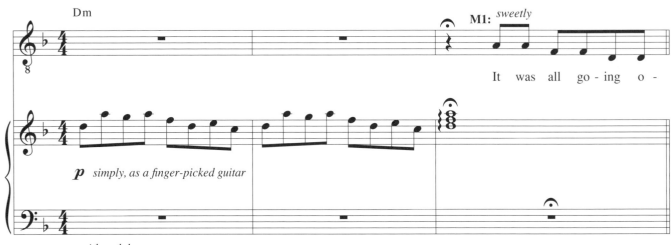

It was all go-ing o-

kay, but now you don't know what to say...

'Cause you thought that you were be-ing clev-er, but you came off just as

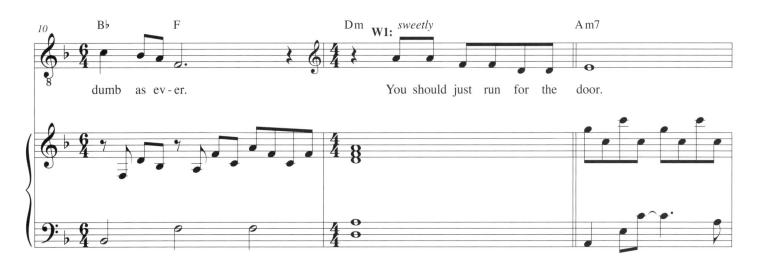

dumb as ev-er. You should just run for the door.

You've played out this scene be-fore, and you're stuck in a

slew of hems and haws. It's so awk-ward... this

It's so awk-ward... this

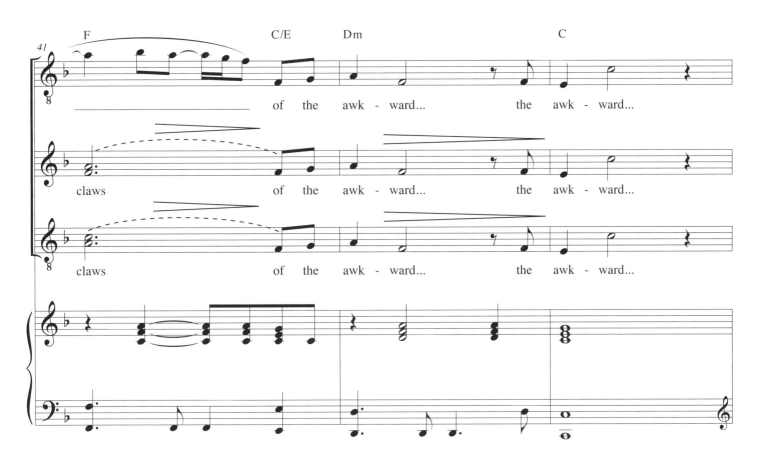

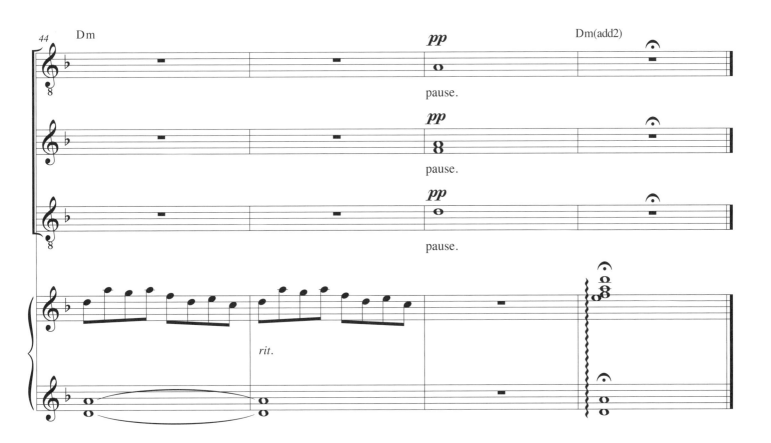

ALLISON'S THEME #1

Music and Lyrics by
ALAN ZACHARY and MICHAEL WEINER

GABE: *Aaron, now's not the time to be thinking about Allison!*

ALLISON: *Guess he can't help himself, Gabe.*
I'm simply too wonderful.

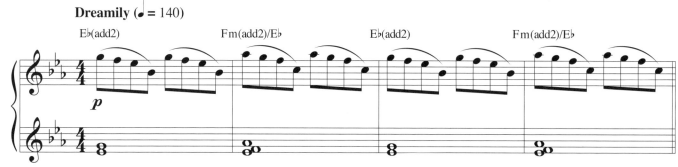

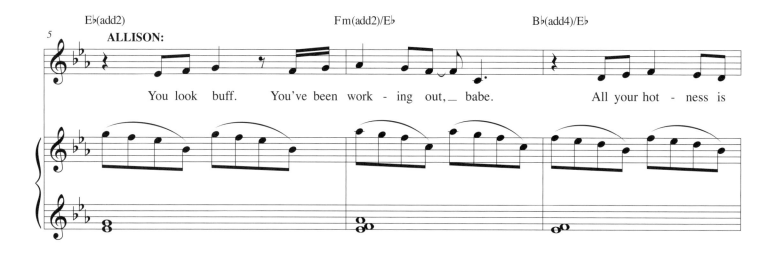

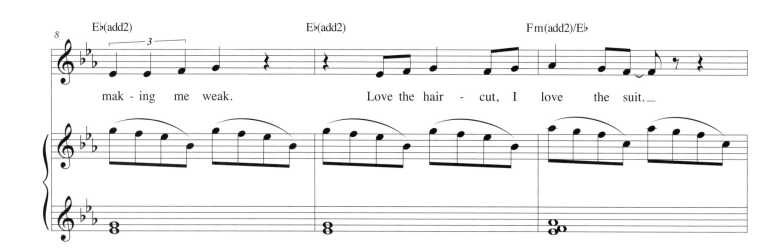

THAT'S WHY YOU LOVE ME

Music and Lyrics by
ALAN ZACHARY and MICHAEL WEINER

SAFER

Music and Lyrics by
ALAN ZACHARY and MICHAEL WEINER

I'D ORDER LOVE

Music and Lyrics by
ALAN ZACHARY and MICHAEL WEINER

Casual Lounge feel, molto rubato

WAITER:

I've made my ca-reer___ as a wait-er. And my job, well, it nev-er gets old. I've seen ro-manc-es bloom, wild af-fairs meet their doom, ev-'ry night, some new sight to be-hold. Yet I

81

ALLISON'S THEME #2

Music and Lyrics by
ALAN ZACHARY and MICHAEL WEINER

AARON: *So who do you have in mind to set me up with?*

CASEY: *Well, that depends. What's your type? [music]*

Dreamily (♩ = 140)

AARON: *Oh, you know. Nothing TOO specific, just, I don't know, maybe...*

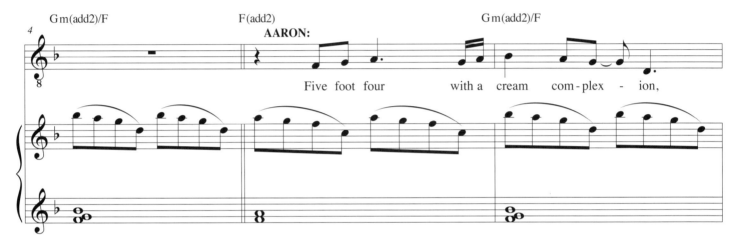

Five foot four with a cream com-plex-ion,

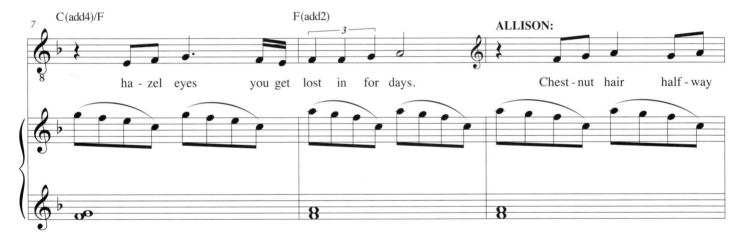

ha-zel eyes you get lost in for days. Chest-nut hair half-way

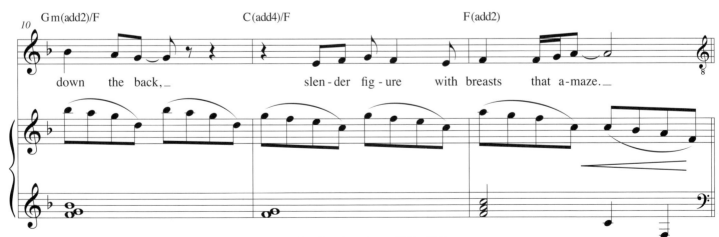

down the back,_ slen-der fig-ure with breasts that a-maze._

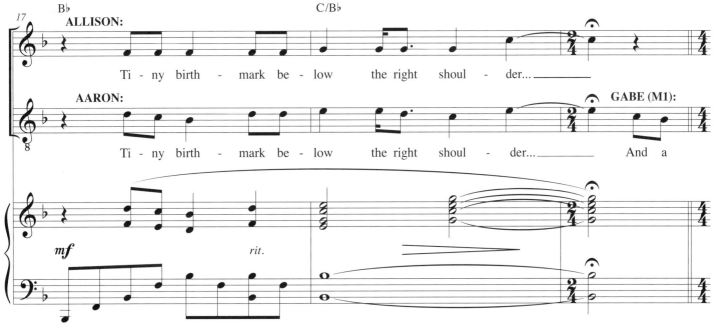

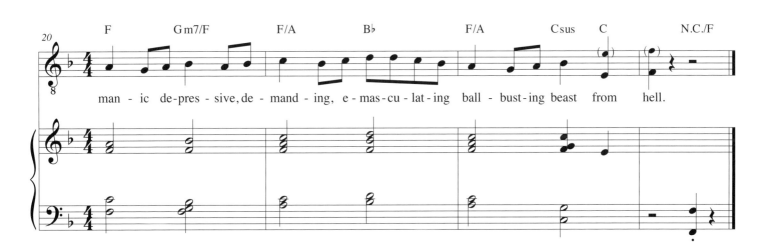

THE THINGS I NEVER SAID

Music and Lyrics by
ALAN ZACHARY and MICHAEL WEINER

IN LOVE WITH YOU

Music and Lyrics by
ALAN ZACHARY and MICHAEL WEINER

102

—

THE CHECK!

Music and Lyrics by
ALAN ZACHARY and MICHAEL WEINER

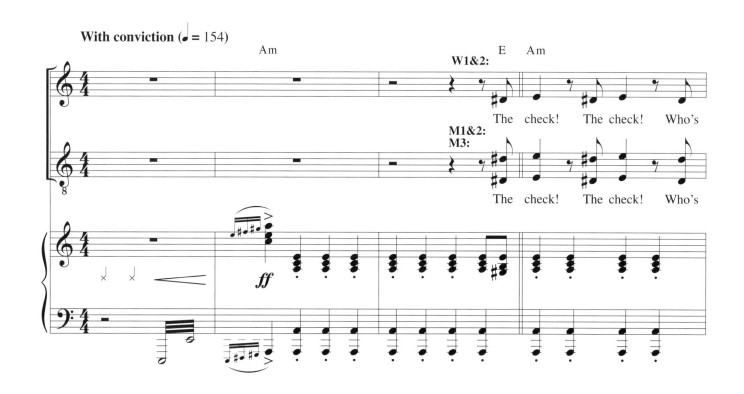

SOMETHING THAT WILL LAST

Music and Lyrics by
ALAN ZACHARY and MICHAEL WEINER

Power Ballad (♩ = 82)

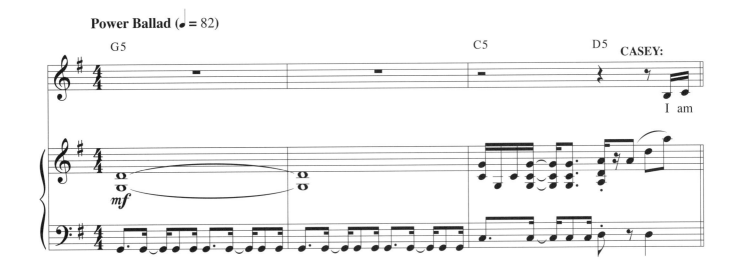